Archibald Keir

Thoughts on the affairs of Bengal

Archibald Keir

Thoughts on the affairs of Bengal

ISBN/EAN: 9783337717100

Printed in Europe, USA, Canada, Australia, Japan

Cover: Foto ©ninafisch / pixelio.de

More available books at **www.hansebooks.com**

THOUGHTS

ON THE

AFFAIRS of BENGAL.

By ARCHIBALD KEIR, Efq.

LONDON,

Printed in the Year 1772.

THOUGHTS

ON THE

AFFAIRS of BENGAL.

THE affairs of India in general, and of Bengal in particular, have fo much ingroffed the attention of the public for fome time paft, and are now become of fuch confequence to the nation, that every individual who either thinks he can throw new light on the fubject, or that he can give any ufeful hints for the better ordering and regulating thofe important matters, needs make no apology for fo laudable an attempt, whatever may be the effect or fuccefs of his endeavours. Seeing many fenfible, and

B

inge-

ingenious men too, who have of late taken
much pains, to point out to the public
the bad management in the government
of thofe rich and fruitful countries; while
few, very few I think, have but attempted to lay down any rational, complete,
and confiftent plan, by which it might be
rendered better; it will be the more ex-
cufeable in me, I hope, who, though I
have made thofe things my ftudy, and
long refided in thofe diftant parts, find
myfelf no ways capable of giving my
ideas in that elegance of drefs and propriety, either in words, or in order, as I
could wifh, and as is due to fo critical and
difcerning a judge. Yet, as I find that
the productions which have the moft of
plain truth and common fenfe in them,
though in the fimpleft apparel, are often
more pleafing to mankind in general,
than thofe which are far more elegant;
and being perhaps fomewhat flattered by
my own conceit, or rather induced, as I
imagine, by the perfuafion and favour-
able opinion of fome fenfible friends, who
have approved of my way of thinking, I
fhall

shall therefore venture, in the few following pages, to explain, what, in my humble opinion, would be the moft rational
and beft method of redrefing the grievances complained of, and of fixing on a
juft and folid foundation the management and right government of Bengal.

And though it may be thought, that in
a difquifition of this nature, it would be
moft proper to begin at the fountain head,
and confider whether or not our home
eftablifhment of a Company and Court of
Directors, or what other form of government would be beft; yet when I confider, that this is a fubject which has already often been difcuffed by many abler
pens; and that it is a fubject too, which
would carry me beyond the bounds of my
prefent purpofe, while it lies within the
reach of every one who will give himfelf
but the trouble to read and reflect; I fhall
fay nothing more, than to declare, in a
very few words, what is my opinion of
this; and that in the moft candid and impartial manner that I poffibly can.

The

The general fentiments then of this, and of all the trading nations in Europe, after repeated trials, and much argument, both for and againft, feem now almoft to be fixed and agreed, that the trade to thofe diftant countries, could, in no re-fpect, be carried on to fo much advantage as by exclufive companies. Though the French are again indeed making another trial of this; with what fuccefs, time will difcover. But the trade *there*, to this na-tion, is now not the only object. For there has of late been acquired a very ex-tenfive territorial dominion: and peo-ple are to be ruled on principles very dif-ferent from thofe neceffary to be employ-ed in the conducting of mere mercantile concerns. It has been alleged therefore, that merchants fhould not be fovereigns; and it has been concluded from thence, that the Eaft India Company are improper to govern and protect the countries they have either fubdued by their arms, or which have voluntarily fubmitted to their authority. The premifes may be eafily admitted, perhaps; but that the propofi-

tion,

tion, in its full extent, fhould be fo, tho'
it feems fomewhat to carry the appearance of reafon, is what I am perfuaded
can never be agreed to, by any who have
the fenfe to diftinguifh the meaning of
words. The conclufion therefore, which,
in my opinion, is abfolutely falfe and er-
roneous, muft fall to the ground of itfelf.
For, not to inftance the Dutch, or many
of the moft powerful ftates in Europe, is
not our own legiflature compofed principally of merchants, and of mercantile
men ? And are not the mercantile concerns of this, and of moft countries now-
a-days, fo intimately connected with
their profperity and well-being, that the
great concern of governments is to put
them on a right and refpectable footing ?

But the affairs of India, and of Bengal,
are the affairs of the nation, and of confequence therefore to the nation that they
be managed well. The queftion is only
this then, Who are the people of the nation, the moft likely to manage them the
righteft and beft ? Whether the king's
mini-

minifters, who can fcarce, I think, be fuppofed to be fo well acquainted with
them, and who have numberlefs other affairs upon their hands; _hands_, which it
would be not fo eafy a matter to tye up
by laws. Or if they fhould be managed
by a fet of men, who, if chofen right,
would give their principal care and attention to them alone; men, who if chofen
right, might be fuppofed at leaft to know
fomething of them; and men too, who
would certainly be more within the reach
of laws, wifely made, and well calcu-
lated for their right government. That
it fhould rather be the latter, therefore,
will, I believe, fcarce bear an argument.

As to what has been propofed by fome,
with regard to dividing the management,
in leaving the Company to carry on the
trade, and letting the Miniftry, or the
Government, as it is called, have the
charge of the revenue, and protection of
the country, by officers named and ap-
pointed by the king; it is a fcheme big]
with fo many inconveniences and objections, that it furprifes me to fee fo fenfible

ble a writer, as the author of the Obfer-
vations on the prefent State of the Eaft
India Company's Affairs, adopt fuch a
plan. The great objection to managing
by a Court of Directors, is, that many
of them are mere merchants, unacquainted with the ftate of India, confined in
their notions, and confequently unfit
either to be ftatefmen or fovereigns. It
is faid alfo, and with fome degree of
truth, perhaps, that their attention,
which is fo much taken up in fecuring
their elections, and their uncertainty of
continuing in office, is a caufe, and a very
principal caufe, of that neglect and remiff-
nefs which has been of late fo much complained of; with, or without reafon, I
fhall not pretend to fay. But as thefe are
evils, which in part either may be reme-
died, or which with equal validity may
be objected to the Britifh legiflature, or to
every order and fociety of men, till the
contrary be made appear, and that it be
proved, that the management would be
better to be entrufted in the hands of the
Government, or with any other fet of
men,

men, I can see no kind of just reason for
changing the mode at present established,
of managing by a Court of Directors.
More especially if it be considered, that
while things are in this channel, the Mi-
nistry will always be a kind of check upon them; and not very backward possi-
bly, in passing any popular laws, which
might help to keep them within proper
bounds, or in hindering any unpopular
laws to be passed, which the Court of Directors, from mistaken principles, might
be desirous of getting enacted. Instances
of which having actually happened, will
readily occur to every one, who is at all
acquainted with India affairs.

Wholesome and just laws are the very essence and fundamentals of all good
governments. For as no civil society can
well subsist, where neither property is
secured, or crimes are punished, as has
been but too much the case, perhaps, for
some time past in those rich and fruitful
countries; so it is clear, I believe, even
without a demonstration, that settled and
established rules, to protect the helpless,

and

and punifh crimes, to fecure both the perfons and properties of individuals, againft the lufts and rapacity of others, ought to be the firft and grand objeft, with thofe who want to avail themfelves of the advantages to be drawn from any kingdom, country, or fociety of men.

To point out a proper method, by which this is the moft likely to be effectuated, is the difficulty ; and a difficulty not eafy to be furmounted. To attempt this, and to endeavour to fhew the means by which we are the moft likely to obtain fo defirable an end, is the purport of the prefent difquifition. How far I may fucceed in the attempt, muft be judged of by the impartial and difinterefted world. For though others have attempted this already, and that many fenfible and judicious remarks have been made, yet ftill there is much wanting, I believe, while every one who has candour and difcernment, or in proportion, at leaft, as he has any fhare of thofe, and is acquainted with the fubject, will add light, and be of fervice to the public in fo important a concern.

C   In

In all ages and nations of the world, it has ever been efteemed the moft arduous and difficult tafk, to form adequate and right laws for the government of fociety. While the moft complete fyftem that ever yet has been made, may in numberlefs inftances be found inconfiftent with the general good, and contradictory even of the very intention for which they were inftituted. Nay, in our own country, we daily fee that *particular laws,* framed with all the care and attention of the moft intelligent amongft us, tried, and rectified upon trial; and rectified, fometimes, a fecond and a third time; yet can fcarce be made to anfwer the intention after all. . Such is the temper of men, and frailty of human wifdom ! As we are not therefore to look for any thing perfect here, the utmoft we can reafonably expect to obtain, in a matter of this nature, is only a certain degree of perfection, which will be more or lefs fo, according to the fober, fenfible, and right judgment that we fhall have made ufe of, in obtaining the defired end.

In

'In framing a fyftem of laws, for any people, or fociety of men, it would be of confequence, furely, to fet out on fome fixed and fteady principles and plan. It would be well, alfo, I think; firft, carefully, to take a furvey, and, in general, make ourfelves acquainted fomewhat, if poffible, with the temper and difpofition of the human mind, fo as to know how, and in what manner, it is varioufly affected. And if we reflect upon this with that coolnefs, benignity, and charity, which we ought, we fhall find, I believe, that mankind, in general, pretty much follow, or endeavour at leaft to follow, their own, or what they take to be their own intereft, and that as nearly as is poffible. The difference between virtue and vice being nothing more, than as the difference between good-fenfe and folly. But mankind are far from being altogether wife. Even the wifeft amongft us is not always fo, either for himfelf or for others. Good and wholefome laws then, fhould be nothing more than the leffons of wifdom, adapted to the meaneft capacity, in pre-

vent-

venting men from hurting themfelves, or
hurting one another, whether by their art,
or by their ftrength. What indeed alone,
and fimply concerns themfelves, or in all
that is within their own breafts, no human laws can, with any juftice, or ought
in any degree to intermeddle.

Thefe are principles, which are fo felf-
evident, I think, that they will fcarce be
controverted by the fenfible and difcerning part of mankind: and they are fo very general too, that they will apply to all
ranks and focieties of men.

Nations, however, as well as individuals, have very different notions of right
and of wrong; of what is ufeful, and of
what is hurtful; and, therefore, of civil
liberty alfo. So that in framing laws and
rules for the right government of any nation or people, if we are defirous of ren-
dering them in any degree happy and con-
tent; their notions of right and wrong,
of what is ufeful and hurtful, or of civil
liberty in general, muft be attended to;
and that not in a fuperficial and flight
manner, but with the minuteft care and

exact-

exactneſs. In ſhort, their diſpoſitions and humours muſt be known; their religion, prejudices, and fancies; alſo the virtues and vices they are moſt prone to, before any thing can be done with propriety in a matter of ſuch delicacy and nicenefs. But the notions and diſpoſitions, as well as the religion, prejudices, virtues, and vices, are ſo very different with the people of Bengal, from what they are with the people here, that to think the Britiſh laws, or Britiſh ſyſtem of government, though the very beſt in the world perhaps, could make them immediately peaceable and happy, is abſurd and contradictory to the cleareſt and moſt evident principles of human nature. And if it be aſked, how then is a ſyſtem of laws to be formed for them? or are they to be left, as they now are, to the diſcretion, and at the mercy of their maſters, which ſome would call their tyrants? Their condition, to be ſure, at preſent, is deplorable, having in a great meaſure loſt the advantages, while they preſerve all the diſadvantages of a deſpotic and ab-

folute

folute government. For while their cuftoms, which were in the nature of laws
to them, are fet at nought; and that thofe
who were their rulers formerly, are now
depreffed, fwarms of little tyrants muft
of courfe ftart up every where, under very little controul; which, of all tyrants,
are the moft cruel and oppreffive. As to
the Englifh law, which has been introduced into fome of our principal fettlements, it is my firm opinion, that the natives there would have been greatly better without it.

It is, however, inconfiftent with the
wifdom and equity, it is greatly inconfiftent with the real intereft of the Britifh
nation, to leave them in the condition
they now are. And it remains then only
to be determined, how, by whom, and
in what manner things are moft likely to
be rectified, fo that a regular government
fhall be fixed and eftablifhed, on a fettled
and folid foundation.

That the Britifh legiflature cannot fo
very properly be the immediate agents
in this, will appear pretty evident, I imagine

gine, from the principles here already
laid down. For notwithſtanding all the
numerous accounts and informations they
have had, of the nature, diſpoſitions,
&c. of thoſe diſtant people, yet, I am
clearly of opinion, they are far, very far,
from having ſuch juſt and diſtinct notions of thoſe affairs, as might enable
them to form a true and right judgment
in a matter of ſo much importance. The
ſame objection will equally hold good
againſt the Eaſt India Company, or their
Court of Directors, being intruſted with
ſuch a buſineſs; over and above what
might be ſaid, in their having, on ſeveral
occaſions, ſhewn ſo ſtrong an inclination
to heap pqwer upon their ſervants abroad,
without, perhaps, ſufficiently conſider-
ing, as is alledged, the conſequences to
themſelves, or to the countries which
were under their dominion. The Britiſh
legiſlature, however, ſhould, without all
manner of doubt, I think, be the ulti-
mate judges and eſtabliſhers of whatever
ſyſtem ſhould be adopted; as it would
be both the moſt for the honour of the
nation,

nation, and for the advantage of all concerned. And as to the ground, on which
I would propofe that they fhould fix their
opinion, it fhould be this :

There fhould be two, or more perfons,
if thought neceffary, fent to India, on this
very account alone : there, *that is in Bengal*, to remain during the fpace of two years,
at leaft; to infpect every thing which
might in any ways tend to make them
perfect mafters of what they were fent upon. And in the courfe of that time, they
fhould not only apply themfelves diligent-
ly to their getting all kind of ufeful infor-
mation, but they fhould go on likewife,
in forming a fyftem of regulations and
rules, for the correcting of abufe, and
right government of the country ; which,
when completed, at the expiration of the
time ftipulated, fhould be brought home,
and laid before the legiflature and public, to be approved or rejected, either in
part or in whole, agreeable to the good-
fenfe and equity, that fhould appear in
all, and in every part of it. And to enable the Britifh legiflature and public the
better

better to judge of the performance, and of the propriety, or impropriety of the fystem in general, and of each law in particular; the perfons who were fent, along with their laws and fyftem, fhould give their reafons in the moft full and diftinct manner, both on the general plan, and on each particular regulation, which people here otherwife might not. fo readily comprehend.

But there being many things, with refpect to the revenue, and with regard to trade, of which hereafter, that might immediately be rectified; they ought to have full power and authority to rectify thofe upon the fpot, by their orders and directions to the governor and council, which thefe fhould be inftructed to obey. What was to be performed by them in this manner, however, ought to be pointed out to them as clearly and diftinctly as poffible, or as the nature of the thing would allow; that more might not be left to their difcretion, than what was abfolutely neceffary for the good of the Company,

and

and of the people whom they were fent
to relieve.

Thofe to be fent, on fuch an occafion,
ought to be perfons of the moft approved
integrity, induftrious, and difcerning. To
be acquainted with the country, and with
the affairs of the Company there, are
requifites likewife, which, I imagine, will
appear abfolutely neceffary. It may be
faid, that they ought to be lawyers alfo,
bred and practifed in the courts here.
But although their being men of letters,
acquainted with civil law, with the laws
of Britain, and the practice of the courts
here, would moft certainly be of great uti-
lity to them in the execution of fuch a
work; yet the knowledge of the law
alone, fuch as is ufually learned in Weft-
minfter-hall, could fcarcely, I think,
render them entirely fit for fuch an under-
taking. Were there three going out
therefore, I would propofe, that one of
them fhould be an intelligent lawyer,
who had been ufed to practice; provided
alfo, he was of good character, as to probity and integrity : qualities, which are

of

of much greater confequence, both in this, and in moft affairs of life, than the utmoft knowledge, either in law, or in any thing elfe indeed.

It would, no doubt, be right, that they fhould be put upon the moft refpectable footing, to enable them to difcharge effectually and properly, the duty that they were fent upon. I would therefore propofe, that they fhould be named by the Company, as their fupervifors, whofe expence fhould be bore, and who fhould have fuitable falaries, affigned them, they not being allowed to trade in any refpect. It fhould farther, I think, be fignified to them, that, as a reward for their merit and induftry, if, upon their return home, it fhould be found they had executed their commiffion with probity, difcretion, and judgment, they fhould have penfions allowed them for life, with fome honourary mark of the Company's approbation and regard.

From fuch an arrangement, and if the inftructions were clear and diftinct, the people who were fent would have no kind of temptation, and would even have it al-

moft

moſt out of their power to do miſchief:
whereas, were they men of ſenſe and diſcretion, they would have it greatly in
their power to do good; and to acquire
both profit and high renown to themſelves, the ſtrongeſt incitements in the
human mind to induſtry and the moſt
noble actions. Alſo the people whom
they went to relieve, would be happy in
the thoughts of the advantages they were
ſoon likely to obtain; and that there was
ſo near a profpect of their eafe and relief.
They would be doubly ſo, were they to
find that men of ſenſe, and of prudence,
who could enter ſomewhat, and have a
proper ſympathy for their prejudices, with
regard to their religion and cuſtoms, were
to have the primary moving and conducting ſo laudable an intention. And the
men of ſenſe amongſt them again, would,
of courſe, naturally open their minds upon ſuch an occaſion; which would reflect
light, and be of infinite uſe in promoting
the general good.

The great objection to the ſending ſu-
perviſors, on the plan formerly adopted,
was

was the exorbitant power given them, and the too little care that was taken to point out to them, what either they were to have done, or what they were not to have done; so that they were left with a dictatorial and absolute authority, without control, both to make and to execute laws. For although it be alledged, that they were just and good men who were pitched upon on that occasion; yet it being universally known, that the very best men who ever have been, and who ever will be perhaps, have their passions and foibles; and that there is not a readier way in the world to spoil a real good man, than by giving him excessive power; so there is no wonder, therefore, that such a scheme of supervisorship should have been totally disapproved of by many sensible and judicious people. With the alterations, however, and on the plan that is here proposed, it is perhaps the only good method, that can ever be made effectual to answer so desirable an end.

As to the plan lately proposed, of sending judges, it appears to me, and to many
others,

others, I believe, to be much worfe than
the former, with all the objections to it
on its firft eftablifhment. For in fending
people of great knowledge in the law
from this, they muft either have been inftructed to have judged by the laws of this
country, or elfe they muft have been per-,
mitted to have formed a fet of laws for
themfelves; and that in a country they
were unacquainted with; where, at prefent, there is either no law, or no written
law at leaft. But if the former of thofe
methods had been adopted, it would have
been entirely incompatible with the religion, cuftoms, and difpofitions of the people. Over and above, that many new regulations muft have taken place, to alter
the whole fyftem of the country, before
that any fuch thing could have taken effect. If the latter had been preferred,
which I believe was intended, they muft
have been fent both with legiflative and
judicial authority; which would have
been entirely repugnant to all the principles of civil liberty, or to any hopes we
could ever poffibly entertain of doing juftice

tice to the wretched inhabitants; which every-body in this country feems now to have fo much at heart. So, to me, it appears evident, that the judges who are there already, fhould we even fuppofe them as bad as they have been by fome reprefented to be, which I am far from thinking is the cafe; yet, being bred, and having lived fo many years in the country, they might ftill be looked upon as greatly more fit to be intrufted with fuch a power, than people fent immediately from hence, unacquainted with the cuftoms of Bengal, and defirous, therefore, very probably, to reduce every thing to their ideas of Britifh liberty, which I am certain could have no good effect.

It may be here afked, perhaps, why may not thofe gentlemen, who are there already, many of whom, the prefent governor efpecially, are well known, and, I know myfelf, to be men of great worth and integrity, do all that is requifite in the propofed plan? And how comes it about, that things in fo fhort a time, under their, or their predeceffors governments,

(24)

ments, should have actually grown, and seem daily to be growing so much worse?

As to the former of these questions, that they should not be so fit as could be wished, will appear from the principles which I have above laid down; besides, that they have many other avocations, which must fully employ their attention, if executed to purpose. It must be observed, likewise, that they have been bred up in the service, and are now the servants of the Company, whom the proposed regulations would principally affect. Many of them too, perhaps, have been long accustomed to think, that power, without control, was of the greatest benefit both to them and the community. It being but too much the temper of mankind, to desire power to themselves, and those of their own sect, although they might be anxious enough, and very clearly see, the propriety of restraining it in every body else.

How that things should have grown so much worse, and should seem daily to be tending the same way, is a matter that

re-

requires a longer difcuffion, and is not quite fo eafy to be made evident. As it is a matter, however, of the greateft importance to know; and as it would throw new light on what I am afraid is at prefent not quite fo clear, notwithftanding what has been fo fenfibly faid on the fubject by others; I fhall endeavour, in as few words as poffible, and in the beft manner I can, to point out what appears to me the principal and efficient caufes; and, I hope, the true ftate of the matter alfo. Were the difeafe once rightly known and underftood indeed, the remedy, no doubt, might more eafily be inveftigated. Whereas, the attempting a cure, without firft thoroughly being acquainted with the difeafe, is acting but as ignorant quacks, who apply their noftrums to all patients alike, without diftinction either of conftitution or difeafe.

The univerfal cry, and what has generally been affigned as the caufe of all the evils complained of, is the bad management of the Rulers in Bengal, and the bad management of the Rulers in Leaden-

E   hall-

hall-ſtreet. That effects muſt flow from cauſes, and that bad management will produce evils, is clear and evident to every body. But, effects being ſeen and felt, when cauſes are hid; and it being much eaſier to point out where there is bad management, than to lay down a rational and juſt plan of doing better; ſo all men, almoſt from the higheſt to the loweſt, looking upon themſelves as wiſe enough to direct others, and having, in their own minds, medicines, as it were, for the cure of all diſeaſes, which they are quick-fighted enough in diſcovering; when things do not exactly go to their fancies, they immediately ſee miſmanagement; to which their firſt and univerſal remedy is, that the phyſicians ſhould be changed. What they would probably next propoſe, if they durſt, without being laughed at, is, that they themſelves ſhould be put in their place. For my own part, however, on the moſt ſtrict and impartial conſideration of the matter, I am far from thinking, that either the gentlemen of Leadenhall-ſtreet, or that thoſe who have had

the

the more immediate management of Bengal of late, are fuch bafe and cruel tyrants, as by fome they have been endeavoured to be reprefented. As to the former, indeed, except a very few, they are but little known to me. As to the latter, I am perfonally acquainted with every one of them, and can declare, that fo far as I am able to judge, they are in general men of as good principles, and of as liberal ways of thinking, as any fet of men whatfoever. That both the one and the other, have not acted impoliticly and harfhly towards individuals, at times, is what I will not pretend to fay; as I know it to be otherwife; having myfelf felt, and feverely felt, the effects of their rigour, and, as I thought, very ill-judged policy. Which I complained of, and loudly complained of, to themfelves ; but to very little purpofe, and without any kind of redrefs.

I do not admit, however, that the evils complained of, have been altogether, or even in greateft part, owing to the mifconduct, and many enormous vices as is

alleged

alleged of the rulers and directors. But they have arose from fortuitous caufes in a great meafure; and from people who had different views and ideas of things, fucceeding quickly one another; applying partial and ineffectual remedies; and fometimes remedies, indeed, which produced effects, the very oppofite of what were expected and intended. A very remarkable inftance of which occurs, in the altering the nature of the coin; which, though principally propofed, and effectuated by one, who I both take to be an honeft, and a fenfible man; yet it has been productive of more evils, than any one thing whatfoever; and evils too, which I am perfuaded will be felt for years yet. Notwithftanding, even of the very fenfible and judicious plan, which, I am glad to find, is now about to be adopted, in order to rectify and eftablifh, on a juft and folid bafis, a matter of fuch effential importance. Another caufe likewife, which cannot furely be called accidental; has been, what in my humble opinion, was the bad policy on the one hand,

o f

of fending the money out, and, on the other, of hindering the money to come into Bengal. The former having been done avowedly, and by orders from home too, to a very confiderable extent, over and above what was exported by foreign nations; while the other was effectuated by means of the large fums of money given to ftrangers, which hindered their bringing in what they muft otherwife have been neceffitated to do. For though it may be alledged, that it was at a time when the Company were greatly in debt, and could' not, therefore, otherwife have raifed the money for their China inveftments, for the fupply of their other fettlements, and for the large draughts that muft elfe have been made upon them, had they opened their cafh for remittances. Yet it being here my intention, only to point out the caufes of the diftrefs in Bengal, I fhall but briefly remark, that this furely has been none of the fmalleft.

But a real accidental evil, which created the crueleft mifery and diftrefs that ever was felt perhaps in any country, was the

two

two years severe famine, owing to the fail-
ure of the crops. And yet this too, tho'
most evidently and conspicuously the work
of Providence alone, has been in a great
measure laid to the account of the unfor-
tunate rulers; for it has been confidently
averred, that they contributed, at least,
greatly to encrease it, by hoarding up the
rice in their granaries, and obliging the
people, dying with hunger, to pay an extravagant price for it. But, unluckily for
those who assert this, while they shew
more of malice than of judgment and
charity; like most others actuated by so
unworthy a passion, they make use of an
argument, which, though admitted in its
fullest extent, must only serve to prove the
very reverse of what they intended to
prove. For although the fact were even
true, which may greatly, I think, be
doubted of; or, if they did buy up rice,
and keep it till it became dear, was this
either more or less, than obliging the
thoughtless multitude, to become sooner
and greater œconomists than they otherwife would have been: the means, of
course,

course, of making their scanty allowance
hold out the longer, and of saving thereby
the lives of many thousands.

Another accidental cause, and a great
one too, of the late distresses in Bengal,
has been owing, as I hinted above, from
the change of the police that has imper-
ceptibly arose from the change of government ; for formerly a nabob, who had
absolute power, could upon any complaint,
and would have been seldom very backward most probably, to call zemindars or
others before him, strip them of their ill-
acquired wealth, or otherwise to punish
them, according to the nature of their
offence. Zemindars, and other inferior officers again, had a like power over
those who were under them. Now, however, things are quite different ; for where
an Englishman resides, a zemindar, or
even a nabob, has scarce almost the shadow
of power left. The English and the English banians, now a days, are the people in
Bengal, who keep the nabob, the zemindars, and every body else in the country in
awe. What kind of people therefore,
those banians are, what their office and

8   pro-

profeffion is, it will be neceffary, I believe, to give fome little account of.

Banians, then, in general, are a numerous fet of people, who are bred up, and
apply themfelves from their infancy to the
knowledge of accounts, to the art of buying and felling, and of trade. They begin
their profeffion ufually in fmall matters,
ferving as runners or under-clerks to Banians of greater confequence. Being the
clerks over the whole country, where there
are no Englifhmen, their progrefs is never
fo rapid. But in our fettlements, as no
man almoft, who has the fmalleft matter
to lay out is without his banian, fo their
firft exhibition there is commonly in a dou-
ble capacity, both, to wit, in that of ferving fome other banian, and in ferving Europeans when they firft arrive, when their
layings-out are not very great. Their
profits, it may thus be imagined, can, at
firft, be but fmall then. The knowledge
they in this way acquire, however, of the
tempers and difpofitions of our country-
men, as well as of our language, is ever after
of the greateft confequence to them ;

for,

for, if by affiduity and attention, or by any more unworthy means, they can but recommend themfelves to one in the Company's fervice; or to any one who can recommend them to a young gentleman in the fervice as he arrives, their fortunes are, as it were, made. For their mafters, if they do but live, and are not very bad indeed, muft infallibly rife to power; when their banians, of courfe, cannot fail to become rich and great men. Even in the fervice of other banians, they often have the art and addrefs to tranfplant their mafters, get them turned off, and place themfelves in their ftead. It is no uncommon thing, therefore, to fee one of thofe, who was but the other day a dirty fellow, at a few rupees a month, and with fcarce a whole gown to his back, become fuddenly, and all at once as it were, a man of power, authority, and riches, giving law perhaps to half a province, and attended too with a furprifing retinue of fervants, and others of his own caft, whofe principles and education are like his own; fo that they are ever ready to obey his nod; and to do, or

F   even

even to fwear what he pleafes. And if it
fhould fo happen, that the mafter fhould
rife to be a governor or a great man, like
a Sykes, the banian, of courfe, becomes a
man of far greater confequence than the
poor nabob ; nay, perhaps, of much more
confequence and authority alfo, that is,
with the natives, than even the mafter
himfelf. But to have people of fuch principles, as thofe muft be imagined to be
from their education and office, in the
higheft departments of an abfolute government, it may, I think, be conceived,
that the confequences will be of the very
worft kind; many cruel inftances of which
might here be fet forth; but that is foreign to my purpofe.

'Another evil, which may be called accidental, arifes alfo from the change in the
government, by which things are become
greatly worfe for the people, than what
they were under their own native fovereigns; and this I apprehend to proceed
from that of their prefent rulers being
merchants, and merchants too under no
check or control, whofe bufinefs and
trade

trade is carried on under the care and management of their worthy and upright banians; people whom I have known not fcruple to make ufe of the troops of the Company, for the purpofes of buying and felling to advantage for themfelves and their mafters ; and that without ever troubling, or, perhaps, even afking the permiffion of their indulgent lords *on fo flight an occafion*, who, it may be well imagined, would, in return, be not over anxious to be troubled with *frivolous complaints* againft *fuch faithful and induftrious fervants*.

Another, and a very principal caufe of the grievances complained of, which cannot altogether be called an accidental caufe, though, in fome refpects, it really is fo, arifes, as I take it, from the unjuft and impolitic ufe of duftucs, perwanas, and chowkeys. But, the better to make the Englifh reader comprehend this, it will be firft neceffary to explain fomewhat of the nature and ufe of thofe, and that with refpect to the former and prefent ftate of the government; from which

F 2   alone,

alone, the effects they muſt now naturally produce will appear pretty evident.

To begin with the laſt of them ; chow-keys are little cuſtom-houſes all over the country, under each zemindar, where du-ties formerly were, and now are collected in an arbitrary and oppreſſive manner. The duties collected belong to the zemin-dar who rents the diſtrict, as part of the emoluments of the land, while, in his ac-counts with the government, an allow-ance is made to him, to ſupport the ex-pence of the chowkey or chowkeys which he either does, or is ſuppoſed to keep up. This charge is certainly a heavy article upon government ; and that it is a great hurt to trade is moſt manifeſt, which is taken notice of by Mr. Sykes, in his letter of the 31ſt of October, 1765, as quoted by Mr. Bolts. He writes there, indeed, of regulating this affair ; but whether there has been any thing effectual done in it as yet, is what I very much doubt of.

Perwanas, again, though in general ſignifying orders, and as ſuch compre-hending duſtucs alſo ; yet are here meant

in

in a more confined fenfe, and as orders
of protection and affiftance, formerly
granted by the nabobs to banians, dalals,
and merchants. They were directed to
zemindars, or other officers, command-
ing them to be aiding and affifting to the
bearer, whether in buying or felling of
goods. Perwanas are now granted for
like purpofes, by the governor of Calcutta,
and by the Englifh chiefs, or fubordinate
governors, within their cwn diftricts and
jurifdictions. Thefe, however, have more
or lefs effect, according to the power and
authority of the perfon, by whom, and
on whofe account, they are granted.

Duftucs, are paffports, or orders for
paffing the goods or merchandife therein
fpecified, duty free, without let or molef-
tation from all chowkeys. This power
was formerly exercifed by the nabobs a-
lone; and that probably very fparingly, till
about the year 1716, that the Company
got their Grand Firmaun, as it is called,
from the emperor; fince which, their
duftucs in Bengal, have, in general, had
the effect of paffing both their own
goods,

goods, and thofe of their fervants, duty-free. They have been obliged, indeed, to make confiderable prefents, from time to time, to the nabobs on this account, over and above the annual payment to the emperor, as ftipulated in their Firmaun.

That duftucs and perwanas then, in former times, fhould have been of the greateft confequence to the Company, and well worth the fums that were expended to obtain the power of granting them, will appear on the flighteft reflection. And that the indulgence then given to their fervants, was but juft and reafonable, can no ways be doubted. They were then only traders, and their fervants were the fame. Even their trade too was confined within narrow limits, and that of their fervants was but very inconfiderable. To get their goods, therefore, fold, and to be allowed to buy others, without being fubject to the avarice and caprice of every petty officer, was certainly of the greateft confequence, both to them, and to their fervants. Now, however, that they are become the fovereigns of the
country,

(39)

country, and that their servants are their deputies and merchants too, whose passion for riches and ambition does not appear to be less than that of the rest of mankind; to allow them such a privilege, to the hurt of themselves, and ruin of their other subjects, is, no doubt, impolitic, and ruinous in the highest degree. It is the policy of every wise government, indeed, to treat all their peaceable subjects as nearly alike as possible; and to render the intercourse between the people of the same country, as easy and commodious as can be. But alas! the present policy in Bengal is the very reverse of this; in so much, that goods, the very necessaries of life, even rice itself, is often sold a hundred per cent. dearer at one place than another, though at not above a day's journey distance. Yet this, sure, can be imputed to nothing else, than to the impolitic and oppressive use of chowkeys, dustucs, and perwanas. It may be said, perhaps, that were these taken away, and it has been so said, I know, that it would then not be worth the while of gentlemen to

be

be in the fervice of the Company in Bengal. This, however, I deny; though this,
I am fenfible, is the only grand impedi-
ment, which ever can at all, and which
actually, I believe, ftands now in the way
of an alteration and improvement. But
if ever it will bear to be debated, whether
the intereft of the Company, or that of
the fervants of the Company, ought moft
to be attended to; or whether the very
being and profperity of a rich and populous country, ought to be put in competi-
tion with that of a few individuals, I may
drop the argument; it being an argument, I am perfuaded, which can be no-
where maintained, but in the meridian of
Calcutta; where, it is true, I have often
heard it done. Here, therefore, I think,
that fupervifors might be ufefully employed, and greatly fo too; and in a bufinefs
which I am of opinion can never be well
performed without them. Nay, were
they but to be fent on this alone, and that
they fhould execute it with propriety and
judgment, the Company would be great
gainers, were they even to pay them dou-

ble of what was intended for their former
fupervifors ; for it appears to me evident,
that unlefs regular cuftom-houfes are eftablifhed, in place of the numberlefs and
oppreffive chowkeys; and that duftucs
and perwanas, in trade, fhall be abfolutely
taken away; and that by people upon the
fpot, who fhall have an authority fupe-
riour to that of the governour and council fo to do; they are abufes, that are
likely ever to remain, till the country be
either ruined or taken from us. Being
thoroughly convinced, that fo fure as
this is a meafure repugnant to the immediate intereft of the gentlemen in the fervice there, fo fure alfo will it ever be
oppofed ; as it partly already has been, I
believe, in fpite of the moft pofitive orders of their diftant fuperiors to the
contrary. Or, were they ever even to
pretend to execute it, it would be done
only in fuch a manner, I am afraid, as to
have the appearance of obedience, while
the evils complained of, would, in effect,
be left unredreffed.

G   Were

Were the regulations propofed, refpecting
chowkeys, duftucs, and perwanas, to take
place; it may be thought, perhaps, that
befides many other advantages, it would
be a means alfo of altering the late adopted policy of the Court of Directors, in
that of fo much hindering people out of
their fervice, from going to fettle to trade
in Bengal. This, however, to me, does
not appear quite fo evident. Nay, I am
rather inclined to think, on the moft ma-
ture and impartial confideration of the
matter, that, except at Calcutta, none but
thofe, either mediately or immediately in
the fervice of the Company, ought to be
permitted to refide in Bengal.

Europeans, and natives of Bengal, are
of a complexion different in mind, no lefs
than in body; timid and fubmiffive thefe;
violent and impetuous the others. That
no laws could, with any propriety, put
them upon an equality, is abfolutely
clear therefore; while it is no lefs evident, that, were it even poffible to enact
fuch, they would both be impolitic and
highly detrimental to our intereft there.
But

But subjects of the same state, and under the same sovereigns, ought, no doubt, to be treated as much as possible with the same lenity and compassion too. The penal laws, therefore, of all countries, I believe, affect every body alike almost; regard only being had to their several stations and dependencies. Yet, to put private British subjects and merchants on a footing, as to penal laws, with the natives of Bengal, even the highest amongst them, could never surely be; without either making the penal laws nugatory and ineffectual, with respect to them, or else treating British subjects in a manner, which, I hope, no Briton shall ever be made liable, or exposed to. To think, however, if they could even be put on such a footing, as to penal laws, that they would be so in reality, as merchants and subjects, is what no man, I apprehend, will imagine, who knows any thing of the nature of Bengal, and of the temper of the people there. For it is well known, to those who have been in that country, that all Europeans, and more especially

English-

Englishmen, are looked upon by the natives like people of a higher order and
rank of men. A way of thinking, which
it will ever be happy for us, and the
greateſt good policy, to preferve and in-
culcate. But they, who are looked upon
by others in ſuch a light; were they even
more modeſt and prudent, than what we
can well ever ſuppofe them to be, or,
than what the generality of thofe who
have been there already, have ever ſhewn
themfelves to be; ſtill, however, they
would carry an awe and ſuperiority with
them, inconfiſtent with equals, and which
none but ſuperiours and maſters ſhould
be endowed with. Were there numerous independent Europeans, therefore,
in the interiour parts of the country, they
could fcarce ever be prevented from com-
mitting acts of tyranny and oppreſſion;
which could not fail to give uneafinefs,
baffle, and contravene all the beſt laid
ſchemes of reformation and good policy
that poſſibly could be thought of.

Few very great conveniencies can ever
be obtained, without fome inconveniencies.

cies. So, although the welfare of individuals, is, no doubt, of the greateſt conſequence to the nation; yet, it being an
univerſally approved maxim, that the
proſperity and well-being of a few, ought
ever to give way to the good of the
whole; I am therefore confident, if it
ſhould appear from what has been here
ſaid, or from juſter reaſons, that the letting a few private perſons go to Bengal to
make fortunes, will be a hurt and detri-
ment to the nation; it will, ſurely, both
be thought prudent, and politic, to debar
them of this advantage, that multitudes
may proſper and be happy. Whereas, if
the contrary can be made appear, it will
certainly give me, and every one who
wiſhes well to his country, and is a friend
to mankind, the greateſt pleaſure and ſa-
tisfaction.

If it ſhould be aſked, however, that, as
there muſt be penal laws, and Britiſh laws,
for thoſe in the ſervice of the Company,
why may not the ſame be extended with
equal propriety and fitneſs to every other
natural born ſubject of his majeſty, who
might

might chufe to refide in any part of Bengal? My anfwer to it is, that though there is no doubt, but what there muft be fuch laws, yet I would propofe, that they fhould be executed at Calcutta only, as is now practifed; where private European merchants, as I have faid, might be allowed to refide; which would no ways interfere with the laws and policy of the country government; and could, therefore, no ways be productive of the fuppofed inconveniencies. That private people, on application to the governor, on account of their health, or otherwife, fhould have leave to go to any fubordinate fettlement, where there was an Englifh chief, to whofe orders, with refpect to removing, they fhould agree, and promife to conform to, is but juft and reafonable, and could never fure be denied them. Yet, after all, it may greatly be doubted, I think, notwithftanding what has been confidently afferted by many, whether or not the permiffion, fo much contended for, would be of that advantage to Englifh free-merchants, in the way of fair-

traders,

traders, as is alleged and ˙pretended. To me it appears otherwife, provided it fhould ever fo happen, as I hope it foon will, that the trade fhall every where be laid open, and be made free to the natives; without their being either harraffed and plundered by chowkeys, or their requiring perwanas and duftucs, for the free purchafe and tranfport of their goods. For in this cafe I am perfuaded, that goods of all kinds, the produce of Bengal; as alfo thofe which come in upon the frontiers, would then be fold much cheaper in Calcutta, than were Europeans to go themfelves to purchafe them; it being well known in that country, that no Europeans of any fort could travel, at any thing near fo fmall a charge and expence as the natives. As to felling goods in the interiour parts, the fame argument muft hold good. So that, in reality, I believe, the only profitable trade for Englifh free-merchants, cou'd only be at Calcutta, in exports and imports to and from other parts of India. A trade, which properly conducted, would be advantageous to

them-

themfelves, to the Company, and to Bengal in general; and which therefore
ought, by all means, to be encouraged.

The next and laft cafe of the grievances, fo much complained of, which I
fhall here take notice of, is with regard
to the revenue, and the oppreffive manner of collecting it. Yet, the collection,
as I underftand it, is made nearly in the
fame manner as what it was formerly:
which, though liable to many folid and
fubftantial objections, has now that additional clog upon it, of being too much
under the influence of Englifh banians.
But the mafters of thefe confcientious
gentlemen, being daily fhifting, while
the putting out and putting in of zemindars, or land renters, is the moft lucra-
tive employment that can be had; and it
being well known alfo, that few of them
are very punctual in their payments; ex-
cufe is never wanted, therefore, either to
turn out the old, and put others in their
places; or even to keep them in, when
the money they fhould have paid their rent
with, is, very probably, beftowed on their

worthy friends, the banians. That the rents fhould gradually fall fhort then from this caufe alone, which fcarce can be called accidental; and that the people muft now be made to fuffer more than ufual oppreffion, will appear pretty evident, without much conjuration, I believe.

But were once a complete furvey of the lands made, and that the country were properly divided, it would be no very difficult matter, I apprehend, to affefs each diftrict, and each village indeed, in fuch a manner as that they fhould, in fome refpect, have the proportioning of every man's quota amongft themfelves, to be paid into the hands of collectors, who fhould receive a certain falary for their trouble ; and were this once but rightly eftablifhed, it would, I am fully perfuaded, be a means of relieving the country greatly. It would afford handfome falaries to the collectors alfo, yet bring a greater and more certain revenue to the government than what has ever been done before. The people would thus likewife know

what

what they had to pay ; and if too high
affeffed, on a proper reprefentation to the
board of revenue, could have their grievances relieved and redreffed. And it
would lead, as I imagine, to another matter that would be of no fmall importance,
and that is with regard to the inveftments
of the Company; for, as the manufac-
turers are in general the cultivators of
the land, the rent of the land, where it
could be done, might be taken in goods ;
in which cafe foreign nations could not fo
well complain either, were the tenants to
be hindred from felling goods to any body,
till that the rent of their ground had been
paid; after which there ought to be open
markets, under proper regulations, where
every body fhould have free liberty, whether to fell or to buy. All which, if once
rightly eftablifhed, would be of great benefit to the government and eafe to the people, more efpecially in thefe times, when
currency is fo fcarce. That fupervifors,
fenfible and difcreet men, would be moft
proper to be employed in fuch an affair,
will fcarce bear a doubt; many circum-
stances

ftances being to be attended to there, which no human prudence and forefight could here ever make us mafters of.

As to the very fenfible and judicious plan propofed by Mr. Dow, which has been enlarged and adopted by Mr. Pattullo, of making lands property in Bengal, I can fee no kind of rational objection to it; tho' this no doubt can only be done properly and effectually by an immediate act of the Britifh legiflature. The Company and the nation, I am perfuaded, would find an infinite advantage from it, and it would make the provinces of Bengal flourifh above every other country in Afia. The execution of it too, to me, under the fanction of a Britifh act of parliament appears both practicable and eafy; fo that I can fee no reafon to urge why the fupervifors fhould not either carry with them fuch an act, or that it fhould at leaft be fent after them fo foon as ever it can be got properly digefted and paffed.

I have thus endeavoured, in as concife and diftinct a manner as poffible, to point out what appears to me to have been the

caufes,

caufes, or principal caufes, at leaft, of
the evils and grievances of late fo much
complained of, with refpect to Bengal;
with the methods by which they are
moft likely to be redreffed, in part or
in whole. Yet, after all, though thofe
have been many and great perhaps, ftill
I am not altogether of opinion, that
they are as yet fo very defperate and in-
curable, as by fome they would be made
to be believed. For, while I admit that the
people there have of late been rather worfe
off than they were formerly under their
own native fovereigns, I can at the fame
time very clearly perceive, that with a little juft policy and good management,
they may not only foon be relieved, but
be put even in a much better fituation
than whatever they enjoyed before: it being always meant and underftood, that perfection, or even a very high degree of perfection, is what I have never yet profeffed
or pretended to. Numerous laws, indeed,
would not anfwer the purpofe, fo well as
a few clear and diftinct laws wifely framed
and rightly adapted to the meridian of the

coun-

country. At firſt eſpecially, it would be
of conſequence not to vex and perplex
them with a wire-drawn ideal ſyſtem, and
multitude of conceits, which could never
fail to diſguſt the generality of a people
who are naturally indolent, and whoſe
minds are not much enlarged; while it
would give an opportunity to the artful,
and deſigning, to practiſe with advantage
the reigning vices of the country, to wit,
cheating and deceit.

What ought firſt, and moſt neceſſarily
to be done, I imagine, with regard to laws,
would be to finiſh the ſurvey of the country, if not already completed, and to get
as exact an account as poſſible of the
number of inhabitants, their occupations
and profeſſions. Pretty juſt computations
might be made of the produce of the
ground alſo, if proper methods were taken
with that intention. When this were
finiſhed, and that theſe were obtained,
it would be no difficult matter to divide
and ſubdivide the country into proper diſ-
tricts and diviſions, in which to eſtabliſh
courts, inferior and ſuperior, at proper
diſ-

diſtances, terminating at laſt in a general
provincial court, and in an appeal to Eng-
land ; though that only in matters of property of a certain amount. For theſe
courts a written law muſt be made, in
which will lie all the difficulty, and
which, according to my notions of things,
could never be done properly and completely unleſs it be begun upon the ſpot
by people of knowledge and diſcretion ;
who, for no ſhort ſpace either, ſhould give
their time and application to an affair of
ſuch importance, in the way as has been
already ſaid. It will require to be as plain
and ſimple, but as clear and diſtinct as
poſſible. Much, therefore, will need to
be left to the diſcretion of the judges,
who, for this reaſon, ought, no doubt, to
be made amenable to ſuperior judges, and
ſo forth to the higher provincial court ;
the judges of which may be made anſwer-
able for their conduct, not while in office,
but before they ſhould depart the country.
On which account, I think, that both
they, and all Europeans in power and ſta-
tion, ſhould not be permitted to leave the
coun-

country till a certain time after their having quitted their employments, and their
returning to the condition of private perfons ; fo that none might be afraid to
fue, and that either juftice might obtained upon them there, or that proofs
might be led in a regular manner, fo as
to appear againft them elfewhere with
effect.

The people being not naturally fangui-
nary in their difpofition, but rather fear-
ful and tractable, they eafily and without
reluctance fubmit to the will of their
mafters and rulers, unlefs when pufhed
too hard ; their ufual remedy for which is
to run away to the neareft neighbourhood,
where they can have any hopes of being
better. Capital punifhments, therefore,
fhould rarely, very rarely, be inflicted
upon them, and that only for a very few
crimes ; for, although according to our
way of reafoning, they may, perhaps, be
juft and right; yet no reafoning, I am
convinced, could ever induce them to
think, that fo many capital punifhments
as are in our laws were at all confiftent
with

juftice and humanity. . Where the ufe of
juries could be introduced amongft them,
it would be of excellent fervice. And with
refpect to property, there is a cuftom of
their own, which has long fubfifted with
them, which, with great propriety and
advantage, might be converted into a law ;
and that is with regard to deciding their
differences by way of arbitration. To
eftablifh this under proper regulations,
therefore, fo as not to interfere with their
cafts and religions, would both be highly
beneficial, and the more grateful, as it
would be a law which they had been
always, in a manner, accuftomed to
before.

As to the trade of falt, beetle-nut, and
tobacco, the impolitic management of
which, as is alledged, having fo much
been the topic of converfation, it may
be expected, that in a difquifition of
this nature, I fhould fay fomething upon
it ; the rather too as I have not imputed
the grievances of Bengal to this caufe,
though, I believe, it is here generally underftood to have been one, and the very
prin-

principal one alfo. This too, it may be thought, I have the greater call to do, as I refided long in the country, had dealt very largely myfelf in falt, and that the monopoly fo much complained of put an entire ftop to my trading in that article.

After all, however, on the moft cool and impartial reflection, I do not think, that the monopoly, as inftituted by lord Clive and the Select Committee, was fo detrimental and ruinous to the country as has been afferted ; nay, I am rather of a contrary opinion ; for thofe articles were not only not fold dearer, but, indeed, at a lower rate, during the monopoly, at moft places at leaft, than, at a medium, had been done for many years before ; while theie was a fixed price upon them, which, no doubt, would have been of advantage to the people, had it been continued, particularly with regard to falt. As to the propriety or impropriety of the Company's allowing fuch a monopoly, and fo great a revenue to their fervants, it is foreign to my purpofe to enquire into it here.

I

It

It is my opinion, however, that beetle-nut and tobacco being the produce of the ground, and in that country, in a manner, as the neceffaries of life, fuch as can be cultivated and raifed in many places where they are not now, the monopoly of them at all is unjuft and impolitic, a bar to induftry, and hurt to the people. The trade in thefe articles ought to be left as free as poffible therefore; more efpecially if it be confidered that they are no in-confiderable articles of export to the neighbouring and foreign nations.

As to falt, it is otherwife; for it is made but in particular diftricts, while every perfon almoft ufes it in fmall, but nearly in equal quantities. It has been the policy of all wife governments, therefore, to draw a revenue, and a very confider-able revenue from it. In fome populous countries it is immenfe, without hurt to the people, or their fcarce feeling it indeed. Why then, that the fovereigns of Bengal fhould not do the fame, without injuring the people in any refpect, I can fee no juft reafon. The inequality of the

price,

price, in an article that is conftantly and univerfally ufed in fmall quantities, is the hardfhip, not an equal and uniform price, were it even greater than what it ever has been for fome years paft. It is the change, not the charge, in fuch an article, that is attended to, and which creates murmurs and difcontent. For, if it only be confidered, that few, if any, eat above an ounce of falt in a day, or fo much perhaps ; let it be fuppofed then, that the price of falt fhould be even at four rupees the maund; but the maund, by which falt is generally fold, is of eighty-two pounds; fo that if we reckon the rupee even at half a crown, which it is not intrinfically worth, here will be nearly twelve ounces of falt for a penny, or what would ferve an ordinary man for at leaft fo many days. It is very evident, therefore, I think, that, in fuch an article, it muft be the variablenefs, not the price, unlefs very extravagant indeed, that can at all caufe uneafinefs and difcontent ; an inconvenience which the prefent mode of carrying on the trade will always be fubject to.

I am

I am, on the whole, clearly of opinion then, that falt fhould, in fome refpect, both be under an excife and affize, which, if inftituted right, and under proper regulations, fuitable to the country and trade, would not only be an advantage to the people, but bring a confiderable additional revenue to the treafury of the government. To execute this properly, however, requires a certain knowledge, and a minute local knowledge indeed, both of the country, of the people, and of the prefent method of conducting the trade of falt there; and that from the making of it, till it arrives on the frontiers of Bengal and provinces under the dominion of the Company, from whence it is wont to be exported, and in no inconfiderable quantities, to the other neighbouring nations. The quantity of falt made in the territories of the Company is immenfe, and might poffibly be greatly increafed. The manner of making it is very different from any thing practifed in Europe, in the way of making falt ; and the tranfport of it, when made, is over an entenfive and populous

coun-

country, and that at a great rifk and charge. There is a fmall quantity alfo brought from Perfia and the Coaft of Coromandel ; but this is very inconfiderable with regard to the other, and of a quality fomewhat different likewife, the former efpecially, which is moftly ufed as a medicine only.

To form any juft eftimate of the quantity of falt that is annually made in, and imported to Bengal, is here what is not in my power ; to give but a tolerable guefs at it, is even what I am fcarce able. All I can inform the reader of it is, that in one feafon, for it is made only at one particular feafon of the year, I made on my own account about twelve thoufand tons, in which I employed about thirteen thoufand people ; and then I looked upon it, that I had in that feafon near about a tenth part of the whole trade of falt-making in Bengal in my own hands. As to the imports from the Coaft and Perfia, I do not think, that, one year with another, they can amount to

above

above three or four thousand tons, if so much.

Though I have already said, it is my humble opinion that this trade could, in no respect, be carried on to so much advantage, either to the Company or Country, as under a well-regulated affize and excise, or what would be something in the nature of those at least; yet I am sufficiently aware of the difficulties that must attend the forming of a right and regular plan for this purpose; and in such a manner as that both public and private should draw the greatest real benefit and advantage from the execution of it. To make this the more evident, and to throw light on what I have advanced, I shall here inform the reader of the whole trade of salt and salt-making, as it is at present carried on in Bengal, so far, at least, as I am acquainted with it, or that I can now recollect of the matter. The process itself being curious, will, I hope, be entertaining, and an apology to the reader for my troubling him with so long a digreffion. It is different

ferent entirely from any of the methods that are practifed in Europe, or from any thing we have any account of as yet, fo far as I know. It will thence appear evident, I imagine, that my affertions are founded upon truth; and I fhall thence alfo be enabled, I hope, to give fome ufeful hints at leaft, in words that will then be underftood, for forming a plan, and a rational confiftent plan, eafy to be executed, which would both be advantageous to the country, and bring a very confiderable additional revenue to the treafury of the Company, and that at no great expence.

The places where the falt is now made in Bengal, are called the jungles or woods. Thefe cover a large tract of country, moft of which was formerly cultivated, and paid a very great revenue to the government, and that not two hundred years ago. They are now, however, from the ravages of pirates, and ill conduct of rulers perhaps, become the habitations folely of tigers and wild beafts, except only at the feafon when the falt-makers

go

gô there to cut wood and boil their falt ; or that either people come to deal with them, or pafs through in boats, in going and coming from the eaftern to the weft-ern parts of the province; there being no travelling there, at any rate, but in boats.

The falt-makers, called molunghys, cul-tivate and inhabit the adjacent countries ; countries, which are much of the fame na-ture with the jungles, only that the grounds in thofe are cleared, and that the falt water is kept out from them by means of banks of earth, which are every year repaired ; they being broke down again in certain places when the rains come on, to let out the water from their rice-grounds, where it would otherwife rife too high.

Some time before the rice is cut down, or about the end of the month of Octo-ber, the merchants who are to hire them, or their own head-men, called holdars, engage the men who are to work at each calary, or falt-work, by giving them a fmall advance. This, by the merchant, is given moftly in money to the holdars ; and that at the cutchery or public office

of

of the diftrict; where a regifter either is, or ought to be kept of every calary, and the number of people who are to work it. The holdar again, at this time, gives, or is fuppofed to give, a fmall proportion to each of his workmen, according to their occupation or expertnefs, in fire-working, wood-cutting, building, and fo forth. This, however, is more commonly paid by degrees, in rice, oil, tobacco, and other neceffaries, than in money; where the arts of fraud and impofition are no ways neglected.

The next advance is commonly made them in December, when the rice-feafon is moftly over. And they ought then by rights to proceed to cut their fewel, and to make the other neceffary preparations for building their houfes and calaries, which is an annual tafk. There are fome calaries, indeed, of a fmaller kind; and near their habitations, in certain diftricts, which have all ready, and begin to boil in December; but thefe having fewer pots, make lefs falt than the others, which are worked farther in the woods.

K   In

In January, or February, when they
get their next advance, every thing fhould
be prepared, and their pots too ought to
be ready to take along with them. Thefe
are made of burnt earth, fomewhat in the
fhape of a cucurbit, and contain each
about three pints, or two quarts at moft.
The calaries are formed of them, which
contain from one hundred to twelve hundred pots each. They are built up with
clay, in a circular and pyramidal form,
the under circles containing the greateft
numbers, and the others gradually dimi-
nifhing, till they terminate in a hole, left
at the top to let out the fmoke. The pots
thus, with their clay cement, form a kind
of vaulted furnace for the fewel, which .
is put in at an opening below, made for
that purpofe; tiles being ufed as regula-
tors, both for this and the opening a-top.
Such is the general form of the calaries;
though fome, indeed, are made in an ob-
long and pyramidal form, but upon the
fame principle entirely; with nothing
more than fome little variation in the fize
or in the number of the pots.

While

While the calary, the houfe they are to live in, and the falt-gola, or place for keeping the falt, are a-making, they prepare the earth, from which they make the lye, to be boiled into falt, in the following manner, to wit: They firft level a piece of ground, and make a falt-pond, as it may be called, from fifty to a hundred yards fquare; more or lefs, according to the fize of their calary; the bottom of which is of beat mud, or clay, fuch as they find by the river fide. Over this they lay loofe earth; to which, at fpringtides, they let in the water, which is falt, to the depth of a few inches. The water, when exhaled, leaves their earth impregnated with falt, which they carefully gather up. Having then prepared a fmall mound of earth, of about four feet high, and fix or eight feet over; on the top of which there is made a hollow, of about a foot deep, inclining a little to one fide, where there is a perforation and reed, that conveys to a receiver below. On the hollow of this mound, they lay fmall twigs of trees and ftraw, to ferve as a filter; and

K 2 upon

upon thefe the prepared and impregnated
earth; on which they pour water to dif-
folve the falt, which paffes thence through
the reed to the receiver, in a ftrong and
pure lye. The lye they carry to the pots
in the calary, to be boiled into falt; gradually filling them up, and removing the
falt as it is made, till the whole is con-
fumed; which is called one boiling

A calary of five hundred pots, properly managed, if I remember right, will
make, at one boiling, full fifty maunds of
falt, of eighty-two pounds each. In fix
boilings then, which takes up three
months, and fix fpring tides, each calary
of five hundred pots, that is but tolerably
managed, will eafily make three hundred
maunds, or about eleven ton weight The
calaries, of one hundred pots, do not
make fo much in proportion; while thofe
of a thoufand, and twelve hundred pots,
exceed them greatly; which is entirely
owing to the number of people employed
in the difpatch of the bufinefs. For a
fmall calary, which fhould have four, feldom has more than two hands; and one
of

of five hundred pots, which ought to have eight men, has not often more than five or fix; while the largeft calaries of all are always well manned, having feldom fewer than a dozen; by which means, the fewel is cut, the ground is prepared, and the whole bufinefs goes on with much greater expedition.

· The falt-boiling bufinefs is moftly put a ftop to, when the rains fet in, which is generally about the middle, or towards the end of June; though, if they have prepared earth in time, and are careful, they may continue boiling ftill a few weeks longer, which is the utmoft that they can do.

The ground where the falt is in general made, and lodged at firft, during the rains, is liable to be overflowed; while their golas, or warehoufes there, are not fufficiently fecured from inundation. The fooner, therefore, they can get it conveyed away to a place of fafety, it is fo much the better. And the people, who are induftrious, take care to do this in time,

when

when many, who are negligent, often lofe all, or the greateft part of what they had prepared. For each calary, in the woods, having a boat belonging to it, one or two perfons fhould be conftantly employed, to tranfport the falt to the merchant who has engaged it, or to a place of fafety, fo foon as it is made.

In the year 1763, I hired of the Company eleven hundred twenty-fix calaries and a half of the large kind, which ought, or were fuppofed to have had eight men each. I hired, at the fame time, of fmall calaries, above nine hundred, which ought, or were fuppofed to have had four men each. I employed to look after them, and for other neceffary purpofes, befides a few Europeans, a very great multitude of boat-men, peons, banians, &c. The people of the large calaries were fo much difperfed in the woods, which are cut by innumerable natural canals, or nullas, as they are there called, that it took my principal overfeer full fourteen days to go round them. The

fmall

ſmall calaries, being nearer together, could be all viſited in the courſe of a few days only. From ſome of the large calaries, I had five hundred maunds of ſalt delivered me. Many of them, however, though they ſhould all have given, at leaſt, two hundred maunds, for which I had paid them in advance, gave me ſcarce one hundred altogether. While ſome, which had had a like advance, and ought not, or had not, perhaps, leſs than five hundred pots, gave me not one grain at all. So that though I put all the watches and checks upon them that I poſſibly could think of, yet, I received only, upon a medium, about two hundred and fifty maunds, of eighty-two pounds weight, from each. From the ſmall calaries, many of which had above two hundred pots, though I am perſuaded they made more than what they gave to me, I had only, on an average, about fifty maunds from each. Such are the ſalt-makers, or mo-luɲghys, and ſuch the methods of carrying on their buſineſs in Bengal.

From

From what I have related of the nature of falt-making, it will appear pretty evident, I imagine, how difficult it would be in that country, to put an excife upon it, on the principles of any excife laws that are eftablifhd in Europe, which would at all anfwer the intention; fo as not to be either oppreffive to the people, or more expenfive to the government, than what it would be worth; or both. To me it is clearly fo; more efpecially when I confider the temper and difpofition of the Bengals; where an army of excife-men would be neither more or lefs than an army of idle thieves and harpies; who would opprefs, diftrefs, and fell their vigilance to thofe who would be ever ready to buy, without caring much for the government, or any thing elfe, indeed, but that of getting what they could for themfelves. And were the excife to be managed by farmers, the revenue would be rather better perhaps, but not fo the people; for the farmers, no doubt, would give more attention to every minute article. Yet this could never be done to

any

any purpofe, however, without an immenfe multitude of fervants, who would
never fure be more tender of the molunghys, or more honeft themfelves, than
what the fervants of the government
might be fuppofed would be. But farther, if we fhould even imagine, that an
excife could be eftablifhed without thefe
inconveniencies, there is ftill another difficulty that would remain, which it would
be no eafy matter to overcome, and that is
what would arife from the poverty of the
falt-makers, and their inherent difpofition
to artifice and deceit; for, as it would be
impoffible for them to pay the excife all
at once in money, at the calaries where it
is made; while the keeping of it there,
as has been faid, would expofe it to be de-
ftroyed; bonds could therefore only be
taken for the payment of it. The reco-
very of which would be difficult, vexa-
tious, and even often impoffible. A faȼt,
which every one any ways acquainted
with the bonds and fecurity of Bengal-
men will readily admit. Yet, if the ex-
cife-office fhould ever once be allowed to

run in arrear, it would be almoft impoffible to hinder it from increafing yearly;
which would both be a hurt to the government, and give a handle to the officers of the revenue, to harrafs, opprefs,
and commit a thoufand abufes on the people.

The plan then, that I would propofe,
for eviting all thofe inconveniencies,
fhould be this :—I would be for having
the calaries let out, in the diftricts where
the molunghys refide, to the head-men
amongft them, either holdars or merchants, and to none but thofe who refided
there; and that not above a certain number, as for example, ten, at moft, to any
one fingle perfon. Thefe might be either
let at auction, or for the firft year or two,
and till that the people could the better
comprehend the benefit and advantage
that was to refult to them, they might be
let on the moft moderate terms; and on
fuch, as that they themfelves fhould ap-
prove of; and that on a rent to be paid in
falt to the Company, deliverable at certain places and times. The quantity of
falt,

falt, that a calary of any determinate fize
can make in a feafon, is well known to
the people there, as well as the expence.
From the larger kind which I employed,
I have faid, that I received only at a medium, about two hundred and fifty
maunds; though I am convinced, and
was certainly informed, that there was a
great deal more made. The price from
me to the holdars, or head-molunghys
for this, was twenty-five or thirty rupees,
the hundred maunds; which, however,
I cannot quite with certainty recollect,
having not here my books with me; tho',
I think, it was rather the former. Sup-
pofing, therefore, that fuch a quantity
may be made, in thofe of five hundred
pots, for example, I would propofe to let
them as above, for two hundred maunds
of clean falt, to be paid to the Company:
the remainder being to remain with the
purchafer of the calary, with leave to fell
it, at any price, not exceeding two rupees
the maund, which fhould be the Company's
felling price. The more too, to encour-
age them, and to prevent their being

tempted

tempted to cheat, I would propose, that what farther good and clean falt they had made above the two hundred maunds, and were defirous immediately to difpofe of, it fhould be taken off their hands by the Company, at one rupee twelve anas, or one rupee three fourths, the maund.

As to the affize to be put on it; having already mentioned the price at the Company's warehoufes, I fhall next proceed to confider that to be fixed on it at different places; which muft, no doubt, be in proportion to the diftance, charge, and rifk of tranfporting it; fo that a fuitable reward may be left to induftry, without burdening the people. And here I fhall only take for example two places; to wit, Patna and Calcutta, the charges and rifk of tranfporting to which I am fufficiently acquainted with. The charges then of carrying it to the former of thefe, I look upon it to be about fix anas the maund. It may be done for lefs, perhaps; but I have paid myfelf fometimes twelve; tho' oftener, indeed, eight than any other rate, when I contracted for the tranfport of it;

where

where the contractors muft always have had a profit. Eight anas, or half a rupee, therefore, I fhall fuppofe to be for the freight. The rifk and lofs is next to be determined ; the former of which I look upon to be ten per cent. and the latter is allowed to be the fame by cuftom. For where the boats are not loft or damaged, which is often the cafe, and that the burdars, or thofe who have the charge of them and the cargo, deliver within ten per cent. of what they received, it is prefumed that they have acted honeftly. Tho' it is well known, that where boats are good, and the people really honeft, there will not be a lofs of two per cent. in the whole tranfport of it to Patna, from the places where I fuppofe the Company's warehoufes to be. Here would be forty-five per cent. on the firft coft then ; to which may be added, for the ufe of money and encouragement of induftry, thirty per cent. more ; fo that the affize at Patna, according to my plan, fhould be three rupees and a half the maund, a price which,

I am

I am certain, can no ways be complained of.

In eftimating the affize to be fixed at Calcutta, I would proceed on the fame principle ; and, from what I know of the matter, I fhould reckon the rifk and charge of tranfport at four anas on the maund ; to which there may be added four, or, at moft, fix anas more for the ufe of money and encouragement of induftry. The affize at Calcutta, therefore, ought to be, at this rate, two rupees and a half, or two rupees ten anas at moft. The fame manner of calculating would hold good as to other places ; it being always under-ftood, that both with refpect to thefe already mentioned, and to all others, no-thing of this kind could ever be fettled with fo much precifion and exactnefs here, as there upon the fpot.

It may be thought, however, that in leaving fo great a latitude for charges, in-duftry, and the ufe of money, there could be no kind of occafion for an affize at all ; as with fuch allowances it could never rife

fo

fo high, but would probably always be confiderably under fuch prices. Yet to thofe who are acquainted with Bengal, it will appear otherwife, and in the fame light as it does to me, I imagine ; for, in a country where power has fuch influence, and that combinations are fo common, it would be no difficult matter, in many places, were there no fixed affize, to get the trade into the hands of a few, and prevent the poorer people from meddling in it till that it were raifed to an exorbitant price. Whereas an affize, as is propofed, would not only effectually hinder this, but rather throw the trade into the hands of the poorer fort ; feeing it would thus fcarce be worth the while of the rich and powerful to be concerned in it on fo bad a footing ; more efpecially as they could never carry it on to fo much advantage by agents, whom they muft employ, as the others, who would both fetch it and fell it upon their own account.

The advantages that would refult from fuch regulations and fuch an arrangement, with regard to the trade of falt, are many

and

and evident; for firft, it could be eafily executed, and at no great expence, a moft material confideration in the taxation laws of any country; though more fo, perhaps, in a conquered country, where the fovereigns are foreigners and ftrangers. Next, I think, none would have any reafon to complain, but rather otherwife; for thofe at a diftance from where the falt was made would pay no more, and fcarce even fo much for it, than what they had done formerly; while the poor and induftrious amongft them might do what they could never do before, make good bread of it, in an eafy manner, by only bringing and felling it. Whereas the molunghys, or faltmakers again, and thofe near the places where it was made, would reap an immediate advantage from it, and have a no fmall fpur to induftry. For, having already mentioned that a calary of five hundred pots, tolerably managed, can with eafe make two hundred and fifty maunds of falt, fifty maunds of which being allowed for the making, at two rupees the maund, here would be two hundred rupees for two

hun-

hundred and fifty maunds, a price much
greater than to them was ever given before, besides the large field that would be
left for the industry of a set of people, who
are of more consequence to the government than is perhaps thought of, or imagined; it being very certain, that if ever
the uncultivated lands, now called jungles,
should come to be meliorated and improved,
it must done by the encreafe and encouragement of the people in the neighbourhood of them, who are principally the molunghys or people in question. For their
greater benefit and support therefore, a
few useful laws and regulations might be
made, touching the wages of the poorer
amongst them, which, I am persuaded,
would be of great advantage to them.

If we next take a view of the profit and
benefit that would immediately arise to
the Company from the proposed plan executed with judgment and prudence, the
intelligent reader will easily see the propriety of speedily adopting it; for, as the
quantity of salt made in Bengal is very
great, and that there would thus four

M   fifths,

fifths, or what I shall call only two thirds, of it come to the Company without any risk at all, and with no great charge, to be sold out again at two rupees the maund; so, if the guess I have ventured at should be in any degree near the truth, it must follow, that there would be about eighty thousand tons paid to the Company, which, only at six pounds the ton, would amount to four hundred and eighty thousand pounds, and which, all charges defrayed, would still certainly exceed four hundred thousand pounds, or the sum that is now paid to the government. The Company would hence too come in a few years to know pretty nearly both the quantity consumed and the quantity made; the latter of which they could always proportion to the former, by increasing or diminishing the number of calarys, or rather, according to my way of thinking, by increasing or diminishing the number of pots in each calary; so that the molunghys, or salt-makers, might all constantly be employed. The Company, from this also, would have it

in

in their power, and, no doubt, ought to keep always in their warehoufes a certain quantity more than what was needed, in cafe of a year of fcarcity, which will happen, in fome degree, at any time when the rains come on much fooner than they are ufually expected.

In the execution of all new eftablifhments, thofe efpecially in which fuch numbers are concerned, many difficulties, and unforefeen difficulties, will almoft always arife; but thefe will ever be fewer, and more eafy to be overcome, in proportion to the knowledge and difcernment of thofe by whom they are eftablifhed, and to the fteadinefs and abilities of thofe whofe conduct the executive part may be intrufted to. That I am thoroughly acquainted with what I have here wrote with regard to falt, is, I flatter myfelf, what will fcarce be denied me. That the plan propofed is therefore juft and rational in all its parts, or that I may have explained myfelf in terms fufficiently clear and diftinct, is what will be judged of by others; and though it is a plan, which, I have the vanity to
think,

think, I could, with proper affiftance, execute completely and effectually to the utmoft of what I have afferted can be done; yet that too muft be judged of by thofe who may fee things in very different lights, and that, perhaps, too in lights, both ftronger and better than any thing I am now capable of difcerning.

FINIS.

www.ingramcontent.com/pod-product-compliance
Lightning Source LLC
Chambersburg PA
CBHW021424090426
42742CB00009B/1243